D0920094

Imposters of God

The William Stringfellow Reprint Series

Consulting Editor, Bill Wylie-Kellermann

The Ethics Trilogy
Conscience and Obedience
An Ethic for Christians and Other Aliens
  in a Strange Land
Instead of Death
  (series foreword by Bill Wylie-Kellermann)

The Autobiographical Trilogy
My People is the Enemy
A Second Birthday
A Simplicity of Faith
  (series foreword by Scott Kennedy)

The Dissent Trilogy
Dissenter in a Great Society
Suspect Tenderness
  (co-author, Anthony Towne)
The Politics of Spirituality
  (series foreword by Daniel Berrigan)

The Foundations Quartet
A Private and Public Faith
Count it all Joy
Free in Obedience
Imposters of God
  (series foreword by Anthony Dancer)

Also (with co-author Anthony Towne)
The Bishop Pike Affair
The Death and Life of Bishop Pike

Imposters of God:
Inquiries into Favorite Idols

WILLIAM STRINGFELLOW

Wipf & Stock
PUBLISHERS
Eugene, Oregon

ISBN 13: 978-1-59752-951-8
ISBN 10: 1-59752-951-6

NIHIL OBSTAT :

    Rev. Joseph B. Collins, S.S., S.T.D. Censor Deputatus

IMPRIMATUR:

    Patrick Cardinal O'Boyle Archbishop of Washington

May 28, 1969

The Scripture quotations in this book are from the Revised Standard
Version Bible, Catholic Edition, copyrighted ©1965 and 1966 by the
Division of Christian Education of the National Council of Churches
of Christ in the U.S.A., and used by permission.

The quotation on pages 25 and 28 is from *The Revolution of Hope* by
Erich Fromm. Published by Harper & Row Publishers, Inc.

Manufactured in the U.S.A.

For Giselle

Series Foreword

WILLIAM STRINGFELLOW wrote a lot about hope. But he did it in a way that confronted things head on. He took sides. In a sense, he was an Ed Murrow of American Protestantism. The likes of him are few and far between, something for which I suspect some quietly give thanks.

The world he was engaged with when he wrote is not so different from ours; the actors have changed (particularly those in the White House) but the stories remain reasonably constant. Nuclear weapons, massive profits and abject poverty still prevail; it is just that now there is more extremity among them. Preoccupations haven't changed that much either. The things that endlessly preoccupy and consume us, and the violence which systemically upholds them, seem at times to enclose the very life and imagination of our church and world. It is these preoccupations, and the "vocation of the church" with which Stringfellow was most concerned, that mark the four volumes that form the aptly named "Foundational Quartet": *A Public and Private Faith, Free in Obedience, Count It All Joy,* and *Imposters of God.*

We could look in many directions for examples of these preoccupations, but as these four volumes are concerned primarily with the church, we might look no further than theological education, sexuality, church growth, worship, trust boards, social services or issues of justice, and perhaps the way the church continues to become increasingly proficient at rearranging its own furniture (the ecclesiastical equivalent of the corporate reshuffle while Rome burns). Stringfellow named those preoccupations biblically as the idols they are. He asserted the biblical proclamation that to live in ways that are fundamentally not preoccupied with God, but with other things, is to live idolatrously. It's easy to see why at times his was the loneliest of lives.

Through his voice of dissent and discontent he also exposed a hope for a world that literally, by virtue of the Gospel, was and could be more than it seemed to be. And he did this in every situation, with everyone: left and right, liberal and conservative. There was simply no ideological position that Stringfellow would himself call home. This, coupled with his resonance and fundamentally authentic engagement with his context, with the Bible, and with the Word of God militant in the world, helps to make him "probably the most creative and disturbing Anglican theologian" of the Twentieth Century (Archbishop of Canterbury, Rowan Williams).

In his writing Stringfellow uses stories a great deal to engage his audience, and that is certainly true in these volumes. These stories were typical events from his life and experience, serving not so much to illustrate a point, as to reveal the truth. They are woven together as his life-work, as you will see in these four volumes. Through his stories the stranger becomes, if not perhaps a friend, then at least someone we can relate to a little in their humanity. There is a great faithfulness and simplicity to that.

Tucked towards the back of *A Private and Public Faith* we find a story Stringfellow tells which I believe retains its significance today. A woman, a priest, the wealthy church, a lawyer, a plane journey, and a tapestry are the characters that form one of the most significant stories in that book. In short, the woman is evicted, the priest rings Stringfellow for legal help, Stringfellow tells him to sell a tapestry to pay the rent, hangs up, and later reflects about what took place.

Now ultimately I don't know how decisive that event was for Stringfellow, but it is supposed to be pivotal for us. The significance of the story comes from the way it is bound up in Stringfellow's own journey (with Christ, in faith), and the way it reveals the true meaning of advocacy and worship in a remarkably simple and grounded way; the truth is revealed in everyday life, in tapestries and evictions. It reminds us about what it means to call ourselves church—the vocation of the church, if you will, which is to live *in this world* where God is.

For instance, in the story it is only when the tapestry is sold to pay the rent that it becomes a "wholesome and holy thing." It becomes a sacrament when it represents "the freedom of Christ to give up any aspect of the inherited and present life of the institutional church . . . for the sake of the world." What gives the tapestry meaning? How does it become a "worshipful" or "sacramental" thing? It is only when the church is free to be poor amongst the poor, that it can be the church.

When someone like Stringfellow comes along and challenges our idols by speaking into a situation as companion rather than as stranger, yet offering a perspective that calls into question almost all we take for granted (our very *foundations* you might say), it is an unusual and uncomfortable thing, and one we cannot afford to simply shrug off. As I've indicated, Stringfellow's writing—the stories, images and language—draw the reader into the text; they have the effect of involving us in his life, and thereby involving us also in the life of faith. I have no idea whether that was entirely deliberate, or whether it was an echo of the biblical idiom that sustained him, but it is certainly effective.

Ethics is enacted in these four volumes through the use of reflection, polemic, and stories—all of which work in partnership to draw us into the world he is engaging. We begin to realize that the world he makes known to us is our world too, and ethics is not about applying some abstract notion of moral righteousness, but about obedience and faithfulness to God whose Spirit animates and sustains creation. His writing models this far more than it talks about it.

This quartet offers a penetrating critique of the church, coupled with insight and hope. Stringfellow clearly expects a lot of his reader, and he worked hard at developing his thoughts for publication in book form. You will see that much of the material for the four books found life originally as articles, spoken word or both. It was part of the refining process, and this allows us to see that while his books may *look* like they were written in a hurry, in truth this was anything but the case.

It is also worth noting that the books came hot on the heels of Karl Barth's advocacy of Stringfellow during his visit to America in 1962, and thus they engage many of the issues spoken of at the infamous gathering, including the principalities and powers. I want to say something about that, and in so doing acknowledge I am going out on a limb. I came across Stringfellow while studying Barth, and I switched focus. I did that because it is pretty clear to me that Stringfellow's theology, expressed through his life-work, can be seen as a completion of Barth's unfinished *Church Dogmatics* (which was to focus upon his doctrine of the Holy Spirit). Ironically, Stringfellow himself died before completing his trilogy on the Holy Spirit, but even so there is a strong connection there. I don't want to get into using Barth as a way of justifying Stringfellow. The two theologies are similar and work well together, but they are also distinct. However, in the American visit of

1962, Stringfellow and Barth spent some good time together and Stringfellow remarked how interesting it was
that they had such points of similarity when neither had
read the other's theology to any real extent.* To which
Barth responded that he wasn't surprised at all; how could
it be any different, for they read the same Bible. To express this with more hermeneutical accuracy, it may be
that the same Bible read them.

A Private and Public Faith was his first book, and
presents a sustained written engagement with American
Protestantism, which he believed had lost sight not only
of the distinct calling of priests and laity, but also of the
idols the church had created for itself in the process. It
represents an early and robust account of his theology of
the church and the nature of the Christian life. In later
books this thinking is radicalized, but never really re-
placed. This book built upon many years of involvement
in church life and governance, and the ecumenical movement in the post war period. It is perhaps of historical
significance that in the preface he identifies his writing as
polemical—something he dispenses with later on.

Beginning life as a book for Lenten study, *Free in
Obedience* introduces the reader to the principalities and
powers and takes its theme from the letter to the Hebrews.
His engagement with the principalities and powers in this
volume has yet to be superseded for its clarity, precision,
and the concise nature of his argument. Many have ex-
panded upon his thinking, but in so doing have not essentially added to it.

The Epistle of James provided the basis of *Count it
All Joy*. Here, Christianity's "critic from within" (*Time
Magazine*) examines the vocation of humanity to live in

---

* Stringfellow at the time had read a little of *Church Dogmatics* and
Barth's son Markus, who taught in the USA at the time, had kept his
father informed about Stringfellow prior to the 1962 meeting.

freedom from the power of death "wrought by God's vitality in this world." We are free, particularly, to hear the Word of God through the Bible in the world. Thus, again, the freedom to *live now*, and the nature of the faith that sustains our life in *this* world, is engaged in some detail. Like the rest of the volumes here, Stringfellow is working hard to re-orientate the church in its practice and thinking from within, and to understand the significance of involvement.

Imposters of God began its life as a study book for high school students (remarkable in itself), and was produced by the Catholic church. It exposes the reality of idolatry at the heart of our common life in the world: work, status, money, race, the church, etc. But perhaps most importantly, it provides hope: a way of living in grace. What is also noteworthy is that it carries one of the very few references and footnotes to be found in Stringfellow's writing. Curious that it should end up here.

Through these books Stringfellow calls us home. Of course his idea of home, as will be apparent when you read any of the volumes, is far from the comfortable pew we often find ourselves sitting in. His words tumble from the pages with the same energy and engagement now as they did when they were first written. The names of people and places may have changed, but the situations and preoccupations remain. The idolatry and captivity of the church is as much a reality now as it ever was. I'm not sure it will fundamentally change, given the pervasiveness of the principalities and powers; but we can hope, and in so doing, live in resistance to their power.

Finally, when you look within these pages for answers, do not be disappointed when you find instead some story confronting even you with a question. Stringfellow was, as Dan Berrigan so aptly put it, "pure depth." Despite the polemic and rhetoric, Stringfellow's writing is neither a fanciful manual nor some early type of Google search engine for the Christian life. Instead he rewards sustained and quiet engagement, offering us an ethic that is at once simple but never easy; he reminds us of the need to be vulnerable to the world and God, and to be obedient to the call to authenticity *just where we are*. He reminds us of the politically and totally transformative significance of the fact that the reign of the power of Death is over, and that we are no longer bound by fear, but can once again live truly, and wondrously, in freedom. In short, he reminds us who and where, in the Word of God, we are called to be.

Anthony Dancer
Wellington, New Zealand
The Feast of St Luke

Introduction

ANYONE WHO reads more than a sentence or two of this book will realize, if he did not know it already, that its distinguished author is formed in a Christian tradition which is Protestant rather than Roman Catholic. Its issue-oriented prophetic quality may seem strange to the Catholic reader, though it is akin to the prophetic quality of much of the Bible. Also, the Catholic reader may miss familiar landmarks, such as certain distinctions between secular and sacred, natural and supernatural, to which he is accustomed in writing concerned with the relations of God and mankind.

However, if we are to make any progress toward unity, Protestants and Catholics alike must learn to appreciate one another's idioms and attitudes and ways of approaching the Christian faith. Doing so will help us appreciate our own tradition better, as well as enrich it.

Still more, this book calls us all to an examination of conscience from an unexpected and disturbing point of view. We are used to blaming ourselves for many sins of commission and omission, but not for worshipping idols. Might civilized modern people like ourselves really be idolaters? Could the Secular City be as permeated with idol-worship as was ancient Rome? If so, what should we as Christians do about it?

One guarantee can certainly be given: no group, young or old, that uses *Imposters of God* as the basis for discussion will find its meetings dull. They might even become too exciting for comfort—and so might the lives of those who take seriously what this book has to say.

Mary Perkins Ryan

Acknowledgements

Some of the material here was developed as the 1968 Mendenhall Lectures at DePaul University.

Contents

Foreword

NOTHING SEEMS more bewildering to a person outside the Church about those inside the Church than the contrast between how Christians behave in society and what Christians do in the sanctuary.

This contrast is not, I suspect, just taken for granted by outsiders as evidence of the hypocrisy of professed Christians. It is not simply that Christians do not practice what is preached and neglect to authenticate worship by witness. The non-churchmen is, I suggest, much more bewildered by the difficulty of discerning either connection or consistency between social action and liturgical event. The two apparently represent not only distinguishable but altogether separate realms: the former deals with ethics, the latter with aesthetics; the first is empirical, the second theatrical; the one is mundane, the other quaint. For the stranger to the Church, to whom the churchman appears to act in the marketplace much the same as everybody else, the straightforward and cogent explanation is that these peculiar sanctuary activities are sentimentally significant—as habit, tradition or superstition—but otherwise irrelevant, superfluous and ineffectual.

More or less secretly, or at least quietly, legions of church people suffer this same sort of bewilderment. If these people sense any relationship between practical life and sacramental experience, it is tenuous, illusive and visceral: a felt connection, a matter not readily elucidated, a spooky thing. On occasion, when a priest or preacher goes forth from the sanctuary to affirm in the world what is celebrated at the altar, he is usually ridiculed for meddling in affairs outside his vocation. Or when, in the midst of worship, a pastor ventures to be articulate about the relationship between ethics and sacraments, his effort is apt to be regarded as an intrusion defiling the congregation's ears. Indeed, in the past few years, during the profound crises of war and race in the United States, well over a thousand clergy have been deprived of their pulpits or suffered ecclesiastical discipline or endured abuse at the hands of the laity for such activities. That fact alone would seem proof sufficient that churchmen generally are as perplexed as those outside the Church about the juxtaposition of society and sanctuary.

The contemporary movement of ecumenical renewal, signaled by the maturing of the World Council of Churches, and symbolized by the changes inaugurated by the Second Vatican Council, has not as yet enjoyed a comprehension among the laity in either Protestant congregations or Roman Catholic parishes sufficient to dispell such confusion. This fact, is not, however, wholly surprising. It should not be taken as too disheartening when one recalls that, from the early days of the Church, the issue of the integrity of the ethical vis-a-vis the sacramental has bedeviled believers and non-believers alike. The people in Galatia were much concerned about the subject, for example, which is the reason some reliance has been placed in this book upon the Epistle to the Galatians.

The following inquiries into favorite idols do not pretend to cope exhaustively with the dialectics of society and sanctuary. They do pursue and, hopefully, elucidate aspects of these relationships prominent in some of my earlier efforts, notably *Free in Obedience* and *Dissenter in a Great Society*, and I therefore regard the present volume as a companion to these other books.

These inquiries profess that a significant clue toward understanding what society and sanctuary have to do with one another can be found in examining the common idolatries of men and also that peculiar freedom in Christ from all idolatries, the freedom in which human beings are no longer slaves, but become sons and heirs of God.

William Stringfellow
St. Matthias' Day, 1968
Block Island, Rhode Island

Imposters of God

Now the works of the flesh are plain: immorality, impurity, licentiousness, idolatry, sorcery, enmity, strife, jealousy, anger, selfishness, dissension, party spirit, envy, drunkenness, carousing, and the like.

Galatians 5:19–21

Chapter One

The Mystery of Idolatry

IN THE contemporary mind, idolatry is generally identified with pagan rites in ancient times or with primitive cultures today. Few modern men in the post-industrial societies of North America and Western Europe consciously acknowledge that they are idolaters. The term is certainly not part of our daily speech, nor do we commonly ponder the prevalence and present practice of idolatry among us.

Yet idolatry is pervasive in every time and culture, no less now than yesterday, no less in Washington than Gomorrah, no less among sophisticates than aborigines. After all, is there any essential difference between middle-class people idolizing their children, as they do in America, and heathen venerating their ancestors? Is the present idolatrous fascination with science significantly distinguishable from the adoration of fire and thunder? Was the ferocious homage exacted by Adolph Hitler less idolatrous than the allegiance commanded by Caesar Augustus? Recalling Hiroshima, or beholding the war in Vietnam, can any of us really believe that Mars has abdicated his throne, or that the cult in which war is the deity, is any less militant here and now than in former times? Indeed, it might be argued that contemporary Western man is more enslaved to idols than his supposedly less civilized counterpart precisely because he is, presumably, less ignorant about the world in which he lives, and be-

CTA as idolatry

cause his favorite idols are the familiar realities of daily life—religion, work, money, status, sex, patriotism. . . .

The Meaning of Idolatry

All idols are imposters of God. Whatever its specific character, an idol is a person or thing or abstract notion enshrined as God. Idolatry is the worship of what man has turned into such an imposter. In other words, idolatry means honoring the idol as that which renders the existence of the idolater morally significant, ultimately worthwhile. The idolater believes that his virtue or worthiness depends upon the consistency, zeal, and appropriateness of the devotion, service, and elevation he accords to the idol. Thus Americans who have devoutly served the idols of respectability and status all their lives feel threatened in their very being when their children refuse to offer these idols the same worship.

In the theology of the Gospel, the event in which God gives and establishes the moral significance of human life in this world is often called *justification*. In radical distinction from idolatry, Christians confess that being justified is God's unequivocal gift to mankind summed up in Jesus Christ. The worth of a man's life is bestowed as the gift of God's wholly gratuitous love for man decisively manifested in history in Christ.

Grace

In this sense, without getting into the controversies of the Reformation, all Christians can speak of justification by faith rather than by works: of a justification at once personal and cosmic, both immediate and ultimate, not exclusive but ecumenical. This justification is unconditional; is not modified by the aspirations or achievements of men. It is not the prize for any accomplishments and not the consequence of any sacrifices. It is uninfluenced by ritual observances; it has nothing, as such, to do with

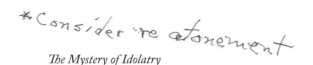

Consider re atonement

piety or with keeping any laws. Undeserved, unearned, immeasurable, free and priceless, justification by faith is not essentially concerned with the issue of the faithfulness of men to God, but with the fidelity of God to himself and to mankind, and thus with the faithfulness of men to their humanity.

According to Christ's Gospel, justification cannot be attained by works of any kind. In contrast, idolatry essentially implies grasping after justification by works of one or another variety—obeying certain rules, pursuing certain values, carrying out certain activities or rituals, and so on. These thus become forms of tribute which men offer to what they have enshrined as idols, and so they become dehumanizing, death-dealing.

This is why the humanist, even a non-believing humanist, can be opposed to idolatry. As Erich Fromm says in *The Revolution of Hope* (Bantam Book, N.Y., 1968):

> . . . the principle shared by all radical humanists is that of negating and combating idolatry in every form and shape—idolatry, in the prophetic sense of worshipping the work of one's own hands and hence making man subservient to things, and in this process becoming a thing himself. The idols against which the Old Testament prophets fought were idols in wood and stone, or trees or hills; the idols of our day are leaders, institutions, especially the State, the nation, production, law and order, and every man-made thing. Whether or not one believes in God is a question secondary to whether or not one denies idols. The concept of alienation is the same as the Biblical concept of idolatry. It is man's submission to the things of his creation and to the circumstances of his doing. Whatever may divide believers and nonbelievers, there is something which unites them if they are true to

their common tradition, and that is the common fight, against idolatry and the deep conviction that no thing and no institution must ever take the place of God or, as a non-believer may prefer to say, of that empty place which is reserved for the No-thing.

As Galatians puts it, all services rendered to idols are "works of the flesh," that is, works infected by death, works leading to death, not life.

Thus the moral significance for their existence which men seek in idolatry turns out to be death. The supposed justified condition—like "security," "loyalty," "success," or whatever—which the idolater covets and pursues in his works is, in truth, a form of death.

The term "death" is being used here in the manifold connotations of its uses in the Bible: not only physical death but all forms of diminution of human life and development and dignity, and all forms of alienation of men from themselves and from one another and from God. Since idolatry of any kind demeans man, prevents him from becoming fully human, death is that which, under many disguises, idolaters really worship. On the other hand, justification by faith means that the integrity of human life as a gift is radically affirmed. Man is set free from enslavement to the work of his hands or mind to pursue his human vocation, to live and live more fully in relationship to himself and other men and to the whole of creation.

Idolatry and the Fall

The attribution of justifying power to idols usurps God's singular office as the author of life; it denies God's place in the history of humanity in this world. At the same time, as we just noted, it diminishes men by the violence it does to the human vocation. Moreover, it radically violates the true being of whatever is idolized: St. Paul speaks of "bondage to beings that by nature are no gods" (Galatians 4:8).

Idolatry thus defies God and dehumanizes men. But it also patronizes and so vitiates what is idolized. For example, where idolatrous patriotism is practiced, the vocation of the nation so idolized is destroyed. When money becomes an idol, the true utility of money is lost. When the family is idolized, the members of the family are enslaved. Every idol, therefore, represents a thing or being existing in a state of profound disorientation.

In other words, idolatry is a manifestation of what, in Christian tradition, is called the Fall. All the tiresome controversies about the historicity of Genesis are quite irrelevant here. In fact they distract our attention from the cogency of the biblical description of men and of institutions and of all creatures as existing in a state of estrangement each from all the others, each suffering from a crisis as to his or its identity.

The Fall thus characterizes *this very day*—or any other day—in the whole of human history—in terms of each man's radical confusion about who he is and the similar bewilderment of other beings and things about what they are. The Fall refers to the ubiquity of alienation between and among each being and all the rest.

The truth of this biblical insight does not rest only upon the authority of the Bible, however this may be understood. It is also empirically verified in every moment and in every circumstance in our existence: when illness assaults us or anger is vented, when a ghetto burns or a rice field is defoliated; wherever men practice idolatry and take imposters for God.

Thus the Fall is about the militacy of death's presence within all relationships in the reality of our present existence and in the history of this world. To speak of institutions or persons or other creatures as idols is to regard them in their fallenness—that is, in such grave disorientation that they are possessed by death. Idolatry is a worship of death in this sense and a concrete dramatization of the fallenness of these relationships.

In the remaining chapters of this book, we are going to examine some of the idols commonly worshipped today. But the purpose of this exercise is a positive one—not to decry work, or money, or patriotism, or whatever, but to aid the reader's perception of the idolatrous uses to which these things are being put in society. In the "freedom wherewith Christ has made us free," Christians should be busy exposing idolatry in all its forms, restoring things and ideas to their true uses and functions in right relationship to one another and to human purposes. But first we need to recognize the idols which we ourselves, too, may unconsciously be worshipping.

Issues for Study and Discussion

1. If, as the text suggests, the profound issue in the Gospel is the existential faithfulness of men to their humanity rather than an abstract faithfulness of men to God, can you think of any persons, living or dead, whose lives seem to exemplify this mark of the Christian?

2. In the parable of the Last Judgment (Matthew 25:31–46) the just are invited to enter the Kingdom because of their works of feeding the hungry and so on. How do you reconcile this with the justification the previous chapter speaks of, as opposed to idolatry? How about the parable of the talents (*ibid*. 14–30)?

3. Can you think of any idol-worship that has proved

destructive in your own life or the lives of people you know, or in your parish or community? Does this help you to see why idolatry is really a worship of death?

4. In this chapter, an idol is defined as "a person or other being or thing or idea enshrined as God." Is there anything whatever in creation which is not potentially an idol? Is idolatry another name for the "inordinate love of created things" against which spiritual books warn Christians, or something rather different?

5. Do you ever feel the need to "justify your existence"? What do you do about it?

So with us; when we were children, we were slaves to the elemental spirits of the universe. But when the time had fully come, God sent forth his Son, born of woman, born under the law, to redeem those who were under the law, so that we might receive adoption as sons. And because you are sons, God has sent the Spirit of his Son into our hearts, crying, "Abba! Father!" So through God you are no longer a slave but a son, and if a son then an heir.

Galatians 4:3–7

Chapter Two

Idolatry As Religion

To serve idols is the elementary response of men to the reality of fallen existence in this world.

The Fall begets the human quest for meaning in existence. Men search for their lost identity. They seek somehow to bridge the brokenness of their relationships within themselves and with others and with the principalities and powers. They grope for justification. And in doing so, they set up persons or things or abstractions as idols and serve them.

In this context, the term "religion" is used comprehensively to embrace the historic and institutionalized religions of mankind (e.g., Buddhism or Mormonism), the philosophies and ideologies which are equivalents of religion (e.g., Platonism or Marxism), the principalities which displace religion (e.g., scientism or racism), fadism or transient infatuations (e.g., the LSD sect or celebrity cults), symbols of security or virtue (e.g., acquisitiveness or status), as well as the innumerable private religiosities familiar to men (e.g., hedonism or astrology).

Christian Faith vs. Reason

Christianity is not without similarities to all these varieties of religion. But, above all such likenesses, the stark, central, and original distinction stands out which sets the Gospel of Christ apart from and, indeed, over against all religion. The generic difference between the Christian faith and religion is that while religion—in the sense in which it is synonymous with idolatry—represents the human response to the Fall, the Gospel of Christ is the embodiment of God's action in the midst of the Fall. Religion is the historic search of men for some meaning in life which surpasses death or, at the least, for some meaning in death as such. The Gospel concerns God's bestowal of life in this world and his affirmation of life in this world emancipated from the power of death.*

Hence it is a misnomer to speak of the Christian faith as religion at all; it is especially a mistake, in my view, to do so for apologetic convenience, though this is persistently done both inside and outside the Church, to the misguidance of believers and the disservice of non-believers. It is, of course, possible, and it is also popular within the churches, to repudiate the Gospel by religion-izing Christianity or by idolizing church. This brings about the condition against which Søren Kierkegaard so vehemently complained in his journals, and about which Dietrich Bonhoeffer was greatly exercised during his imprisonment. The perversion of the Gospel into what would later be called "Christendom" is a principal concern of Galatians; it remains a besetting affliction in the American sects and denominations today. Still, that the churches can be made into idols or that Christianity can be misconstrued as religion does not either vitiate the Church of Christ or neutralize the Gospel of Jesus Christ. It rather emphasizes the pathos of being a Christian in the world as it is.

---

* An extensive treatment of the contrast of the Christian faith and religion is contained in this author's book, *Count It All Joy* (Wipf and Stock, 1967).

Idolatry and Pantheism

This world as it is harbors a grotesque array of idols. They are legion. Apart from their common attribute as surrogates of death, they vary much in character, appearance, tenure and power. Some idols seem noble—as, say, democracy does—while others are notoriously base—like Nazism, for example. Again, the idolatry of alumni for an alma mater may appear innocuous, yet it can be more ferocious than some others because it exploits sentimentality at the expense of reason. In American folklore, the family is upheld as a benign idol for the middle classes, though the poor suffer atrociously directly in consequence of this idolatry—as the public school situation in a score of cities illustrates.

Sometimes it seems as if there were some strange hierarchy of idols, as when patriotism is set above all other allegiances in wartime. But this, too, is more a question of the idolizers than of the idols. Thus, the American entrepreneurs who have profiteered so immensely from the conflict in Vietnam evidently esteem money more than country, or more than what has been promulgated officially as the patriotic cause.

At the same time, there appears to be some qualitative differences among current idols. Some, like education, have an institutional character, while others, like racism, are ostensibly ideological. But, I believe, the two cannot be effectively separated. Ideology is inherent in every institution, while institutional forms are implied in every ideology—and both actually represent components of the reality of every idol. Our worship of "education," for example, regardless of its quality or effectiveness in developing human potentialities, clearly has many ideological components, including the worship of middle-class values good and bad, and of an egalitarian type of democracy. It also has vast and complex institutional components, including its relationship to government, industry, and the labor market.

This multiplicity and variety of idols means that each idol is a competitor with all other idols for the very lives of men. The old sayings about jealousies among the gods express this competition. The insatiable need of each idol for worship—for tribute to its claim of sovereignty or justifying power—is identical with the pretension of every idol to be the true god. Nevertheless, idols can be readily discerned acting in concert, aiding and abetting one another. The idol of sports illustrates how this occurs, notably where zealous attention to sports distracts people from the wiles of other idols. It is not just happenstance that the most totalitarian racist regime in the world—South Africa—is so passionate about athletics. It is no mere coincidence that it was during the 1967 World Series in America that the Pentagon was engaged in determining the contingent assignments of federal military forces for riot duty in the cities.

The turmoil of the relationships among the diverse idols emphasizes the erratic nature of human idolatry. Men switch their idols constantly. What may be an assertedly ultimate devotion at the moment is not necessarily so regarded later on. Indeed, it is seldom, if ever, the case that a man serves only one idol at a time. Rather the idolater offers his tribute to a host of idols simultaneously, all of them remaining in essential conflict with one another. At home, the family is apt to reign, or the idol named posterity; but on the job, work itself may be idolized, or corporation, or union, or art, or profession. More privately, the same person who worships these idols may also serve acquisitiveness or his own image as an idol and, if he goes to a church, it is more likely than not that this is for him another form of idolatry.

Thus idolatry means more than that men are religious. It means that they are religious in a peculiar way: they are pantheists. The contemporary, Western, urban man is in truth as much a pantheist as any Greek or any Inca. Discussions about "secularism"—whether for it or against it—would be more realistic if they took this fact into account.

Issues for Study and Discussion

1. Could it be said that every prejudice is the effect of some form of idolatry? Give examples.

2. Read or re-read Arthur Miller's play *Death of a Salesman*. Does this chapter's discussion of idols shed any light on his tragedy? Do the same with Salinger's *Catcher in the Rye* or any other novel or play dealing with current issues.

3. What would you say are the dominant idols of the two major political parties in this country?

4. Can "student unrest" be interpreted as a revolt against established idols? If so, are the students in danger of becoming enslaved to some other idols?

5. Would you say that any idolatry was involved in the school-prayer issue? In the question of public aid to church-related schools? On one side or on both?

Do not be deceived; God is not mocked, for whatever a man sows, that he will also reap. For he who sows to his own flesh will from the flesh reap corruption; but he who sows to the Spirit will from the Spirit reap eternal life.

Galatians 6:7–8

Chapter Three

Idolatry In Work

N O SPECIFIC form of idolatry is more commonly indulged in, more typical of all idolatries, or more literally an enactment of the futility of "justification by works" than the idolatry of work in our society. The same is true of similar societies first spawned in the industrial revolution and now suffering the upheavals occasioned by urbanization and advanced technologies. No form of idolatry is more cynically practiced or more empirically corrupted, though perhaps none is so clothed in romantic shibboleth. None is more alien to biblical insight either. In such societies, no favorite idol is more blatantly a symbol of death than the ethic of work, and no popular idolatry is more poignantly a worship of death than the activity called work.

The myth on which the worship of work is based is that in the occupation of work itself—in the mere doing of it—as well as in the products of work or in the rewards of work, a man's existence is morally vindicated. Work is the way, it is supposed, that a man proves his virtue. Work is beheld as intrinsically worthwhile, and most especially so if it enhances a person's wealth, influence, or reputation. Immortality is even attributed to some men because their work has been remembered after they have died (usually because the dead have left a large estate or endowment or some similar monument), and the patent incredibility of such assertions is seldom recognized and never ridiculed.

The idea that work is inherently good, in the sense of being self-justifying for the worker, is fancied among many professed Christians. It has long been prominent, for instance, in the lexicon of Calvinist pietism. It was promulgated as part of the schema of Puritan rectitude. It sometimes found favor among clergy shepherding new immigrants to North America because it facilitated their economic and cultural assimilation. It lingers in vogue today among those who fondly preach that any man of adequate health, pliable conscience, "positive thought," and an aggressive spirit can do or be or have anything he wants.

Even though churchmen have been much beguiled by this work ethic, it is of distinctly secular, not Christian, and emphatically not biblical, origins. Thus, in the days of feudalism, a doctrine of work developed which readily rationalized the exploitation of the peasantry and offered them the fearsome comfort that their bondage to work was ordained to be the means of their salvation. In the settlement of the American frontier and, later on, in the era of primitive industrialization, this same concept of work sponsored the illusion that men can be sovereign in history if they but muster the will to exert dominion over the rest of creation. Salvation through work was a propitious proposition for laissez faire capitalism as well. It simultaneously furnished entrepreneurs with a seemingly unassailable alibi for the exploitation of both natural resources and human beings, and served to keep the laborers humble, dutiful, and grateful. Nowadays a version of this ethic of work is invoked to extenuate the suppression of black citizens in the United States.

The Biblical Descriptions of Work

That sometimes this secular doctrine of work has received sanction as Christian can only be regarded as an aberration because the biblical understanding of work is so contrary to it. Work is described in the Bible as the broken relationship between men and the rest of creation. Work is the biblical designation for men's lost dominion over creation. Work (as distinguished from man's proper charge to "fill the earth and have dominion over it," "to till the garden and to keep it") refers to the reality, in the Fall (that is, in this history), of the enslavement of men to institutions and similar principalities, and to nature. Such is the description of work in Genesis and such it is elsewhere throughout the biblical witness (see Genesis 3:17–19, cf.).

The essential meaning of the rupture of relationships between men and the rest of creation which constitute work is death. Men die, and all their activity as work dies even as it is conceived and then done, and all the products and any of the rewards of work die too. In work, men are not in the position of masters or heirs, as Galatians puts it, but in that of slaves whose toil is powerless to free them from death. Despite all the ingenious pretensions and vain rationalizations to the contrary, men, according to the Bible, quite literally work to death.

The biblical identification of work as the expression of the alienation of men from the rest of creation covers not only work in the ordinary connotations of a job or occupation, but also all the forms of non-work as they are usually regarded. Thus, leisure time and its manifold uses, voluntary or compulsory retirement, unemployment and unemployability, certain criminal ventures, the occupations and pastimes common to childhood and adolescence, the status of economic independence (as with inherited wealth), or that of economic dependence (as with welfare recipients), study, charitable endeavors for both donors and beneficiaries, and uncompensated activities of all sorts, like housework or hobbies—all these are concrete examples of the same broken relationship which men suffer in work. Each embodies the same meaning of death. Each is as dehumanizing and as enslaving as work is. None offers actual escape from the burden of work for men in this world. Non-work represents the same idolatry as work.

Emperical Verification of the Biblical Insight

That work is idolatrous—that work is a worship of death disguised as an ethic of justification for men, and that the various forms of non-work paradoxically share the essential character of work—is not only the biblical view. It is verified in the everyday experience of men at work.

The sheer unremitting harshness of work for the vast multitudes of human beings, both long ago and in the present time, in the so-called underdeveloped regions of the earth is obvious. The presence of death in work is clearly to be seen in the poverty, disease, deprivation and coercion which is the most typical condition of human life in this world. The same presence may be perceived in the supposedly advanced societies among the urban poor, migrant laborers, the unemployed, those displaced by technological change, military conscripts. But it is also to be found among the employed and prosperous as well.

The latter are comparatively a tiny minority of mankind, but their status and affluence have not made them free from the presence of death in their work. The demands of conformity in thought, deed, and word, the surveillance of dress, social life and the use of time, the human attrition which is the cost of "success"—these are all familiar threats of death in work. In fact, the idolatry implicit in the occupations of the prosperous is intensified because their work not only enslaves them but also is parasitical in relation to the dispossessed of the earth. All that the poor have denied them is thereby supplied to the middle class and the rich, and thus the lives of the poor subsidize the existence of the prosperous.

The notion exists, of course, that even though work may be as enslaving for the privileged as it is for the masses of the unprivileged, at least some few occupations or activities are different and nobler. Artists, for example, are thought to be freer than "wage slaves" or the servants of corporations, and so somehow are exempted from the burden of death in work. The same freedom is often affirmed, for example, about teaching or medicine and the other self-styled serving professions. Yet because the appeal of these fields is almost invariably presented as the gain of some sense of personal satisfaction for the practitioner, they hold no special virtue; indeed, no virtue at all, they represent only somewhat more beguiling forms in which idolatry in work claims to justify the worker. Theologically, their practitioners are in the same situation as the man who supposes that his moral worth is proved in proportion to the scale of compensation he receives or the property he controls or the celebrity or power which attaches to his work.

Work can be redeemed from idolatry. But this redemption is not achieved by the particular kind of work in which a person engages, and not by any circumstance of choice in work, and not by the competence or zeal with which work may be prosecuted. Work is redeemed from idolatry only when the worker realizes the freedom from the power of death given by the affirmation of life as a gift. Then work becomes a celebration and use of that freedom.

Issues for Study and Discussion

1. Is the work ethic in American society changing as advanced technology displaces human labor? Would the proposed "guaranteed annual wage" alter the ethic of work?

2. Return to the parable of the Last Judgment in Matthew 21. How are the just free from the idolatry of work in their feeding of the hungry and so on? Does the statement (1 John 3:14), "We know that we have passed out of death into life, because we love the brethren" shed any light on this question?

3. The word "service" is used both for forms of worship and of the Christian's duty toward his fellowmen. How does either form of service differ from the idolatry of work described in this chapter?

4. Does this chapter imply that there is no ultimate use in improving working conditions, doing away with degrading forms of work, eliminating physical toil and the other possibilities increasingly available to make human work less "deadly"?

For if any one thinks he is something, when he is nothing, he deceives himself.

Galatians 6:3

Chapter Four

Money and Status As Idols

INTIMATELY ASSOCIATED—INDEED, often inextrica-
bly implicated—with idolatry in work are the idols of
money and status. This bond is especially evident in post-
industrial societies with respect to work narrowly construed as any compensated occupation (as distinguished
from the biblical description of work as representing the
broken relationship between men and the rest of creation—a description which embraces work in its narrow
sense and the several varieties of non-work as well). Here
attention is focused less upon the performance of the activities called work than upon what such activities yield as
rewards or satisfactions, which are also considered prime
motivations for engaging in them.

The most common of these considerations is money
and the things which money can purchase or procure, and
the status of one sort or another which may be a dividend
of the acquisition, possession or expenditure of money, or
sometimes a substitute for monetary compensations.

In speaking of either money or status, our concern
is not merely with the greedy love of lucre or with the
pursuit of celebrity or other social recognition as self-ag-
grandizement. Such excesses, of course, clearly illustrate
idolatry of money or status or both. But so do the much
more modest, familiar and apparently attractive senti-
ments expressed as philanthropy, the desire for security or

the honoring of posterity. Where money or status as idols is concerned, the case of Ebinezer Scrooge is relevant; but the far more frequent example of keeping up with the Jones' is much more relevant because more typical.

In the extraordinary circumstances like those of the miser, as well as in the commonplace like those portrayed in, say, *Better Homes & Gardens*, the issue remains the same. In both cases, the acquisition and uses of money and/or the attainment and exercises of status are sought idolatrously, that is, as furnishing moral vindication, as demonstrative of virtue, as self-justifying. Consider, for example, some ordinary situations where money or status or the two in association are involved.

Idolatry in Conventional Charity

Organized charity, perhaps because it has become engineered after the manner of business enterprise and because of the intense competition for donations, is notorious in American society for its appeals to justification by works rather than the meeting of human needs. Funds solicitation is now almost universally pitched to gaining support for a given charity as a means by which the donor will gain some feeling of satisfaction, evidence of his community responsibility. Or otherwise receive reassurance of his moral worth. That the charity nominally designates some disease, deprivation or social problem is quite secondary, and increasingly infrequent aspect of institutionalized charity. And well that might be, when it is also taken into account that as much as sixty cents of every donated dollar may be actually spent on promotion, fund raising, and administrative overhead rather than research, construction, or care.

In fact, the indoctrination of donors in the idea that the reason to support a charity is some sense of justification for the donor, and not essentially to help or heal or comfort another human being, has become so successfully imbued that some organized charities designed originally to meet needs which have now ceased to exist in a substantial way, nevertheless continue to flourish because they have a constituency habituated to give regardless of empirical need. In such circumstances, charitable giving may not be effective, but might seem harmless enough. In reality it is perilous for the donor just because it is so blatantly idolatrous.

Some aspects of organized charity make little or no pretense that indulgence in charitable works is for any other substantial reason than the enhancement of the public reputation or social status of the company or person involved. For multitudes of firms both great and small, support of charity is openly recognized as a public relations expense or an investment in future business prospects, conveying at the same time tax advantages. The charitable enterprises of the Junior League variety are no less status seeking. Similar self-justifying ego interests are almost inevitably present in other forms of philanthropy, especially in the endowing of monuments or other works after the decease of the benefactor. Few charitable endeavors are free from idolatrous implications, as is witnessed by the recruitment appeals for the Peace Corps and for Visita, both of which began with some naivité in this regard but now are geared emphatically to the line that volunteers for these efforts can thus accomplish their own moral justification.

The Search for Security

The acquisition and control (not necessarily ownership) of money and the inheritance or attainment of status in the class structure are popularly regarded as the equivalents of security for a person or family. "Security" in this context is a transparent euphemism for justification by works and thus idolatry is disguised in such pursuits. And, as death is present in all species of idolatry, so it is here, often in literal terms.

I am well acquainted, for instance, with a certain suburban family in Massachusetts, a very status-conscious household. Some years ago on the very same day that the husband and father was elected to the vestry of a congregation to which the family belonged, he signaled his newly advanced social position by trading in his Chevrolet for an Oldsmobile. One might count the status anxiety of the parent as trivial if it did not have such deadly consequences. The eldest son of the family, who is to be graduated from high school this year, recently confided in me that he was confronted with a dilemma occasioned by his parents' insistence that he go to college. The boy is bright enough for college work, but is adamant that he does not want to go to college. He has a strong mechanical aptitude and an enthusiasm for cars and wants to be an automobile mechanic; perhaps, someday, having his own business and owning his own garage. His is a realistic and attainable ambition, for which he sees no necessity or advantage in going to college. But his parents are firm. Not only must he attend college, it is mightily important to them that he be admitted to a certain kind of college—Wesleyan or Amherst, say, rather than Northeastern University or the University of Bridgeport. They feel, he discerns, that they will somehow suffer a loss of face if he does not do so. Thus coerced by parental idolatry of status, he contemplates a drastic action to assert and defend his integrity as a person. He proposes presently to enlist in the Marines, quite aware of the wartime risks that this entails, in the hope that, if he survives his enlistment, he will be freed from enrolling in college as a status obligation.

The factitious aspects of the quest for security in status or money are evidenced in many other ways. Where security is in reality a synonym for conformity in opinion, conduct, dress, or custom that is the case. The contemporary hippie movement is a pointed example because it ostensibly protests the ethics of conformity of white middle-class society. Yet it offers only another style of conformity which is, if anything, more rigid, inverted and bereft of social conscience than that against which it complains with such disillusionment, imagination and poignancy. Any conformity, including that suffered in the name of non-conformity, embodies status as an idol.

The Promise of Immortality

The idolatry of money and status have their most bizarre and ludicrous form as a promise of immortality. Wealth and reputation are taken as evidence, not simply of the virtue of a man during his life but as the measure of the moral worth of his life after death. Conspicuous illustrations of this notion of immortality occur when a person's death leaves a substantial estate or surviving works of any sort, like a business with which he was associated, his ideas, his philanthropy, his inventions. Though the man dies, it seems that he achieves some transcendence over the power of death, an immortality, because of such residues of his life. It is a fragile immortality; indeed, subjected itself to death, for it consists of nothing more enduring than the memories of others. As every man dies, so everything any man has said or thought or done dies also, and the remembrance of all that dies as well; and if these things do not die on the day of his death, they die soon enough thereafter. This is not only an issue for the rich or famous, however. The same illusion of immortality is held out to others by insurance promotion, urging them to succumb to commercial appeals to seek their own justification by working for the sake of their posterity. Among the middle class, at least, few escape the enticement to idolize money and status as a vain assurance of immortality.

But Christians should be able to see clearly that such a promise of immortality, along with the search for security in money or status, or the idolatry typical of the works of conventional charity, neither prevail against the power of death hereafter nor, what is more significant, here and now.

Issues for Study and Discussion

1. In modern society is it possible to engage in any charitable endeavors that are not corrupt?
2. Can you relate the problem of the futility of seeking "security" in status to the issue of a man's faithfulness to his humanity, raised in Chapter One?
3. Do you think that our economy would collapse if people generally stopped idolizing work, money, and status?
4. Do you know of any persons who have enough money to live without working, who are working for other reasons than status or self-justification?

For you were called to freedom, brethren; only do not use your freedom as an opportunity for the flesh, but through love be servants of one another. For the whole law is fulfilled in one word, "You shall love your neighbor as yourself." But if you bite and devour one another take heed that you are not consumed by one another.

Galatians 5:13–15

Chapter Five

The Idolatry of Race

J USTIFICATION BY works, which inheres in every idolatry, may appear to represent a primary individualistic
relationship where idols like money or status are concerned, but the same theological issue is present where a
whole class or race of people are possessed by an idol.

The notorious instance of such mass idolatry in
the Western nations today is American white supremacy. Racism is not novel to the American experience, of
course, since it has been, and remains, familiar in virtually
all places in which Anglo-Saxons have been indigenous
or have become settlers. Still, racism has a particular significance in the American context if only because of the
military and economic pre-eminence of the power of the
United States in the world. Racism is no less virulent in
Rhodesia than in America, but it is of relatively less influence because white Rhodesia is a power of far less consequence.

Many white Americans harbor the impression that
the racial crisis is of recent origin, having suddenly broken
on the scene during the past fifteen years or so, rupturing
the peaceable relations of whites and blacks and interrupt-
ing the steady improvement of those relationships from
generation to generation. In truth, racism originated in
America three and a half centuries ago—in 1619, when
a Portuguese trader sold some black men into chattel

slavery to some early white settlers in Virginia. From that time to the present day, white supremacy has been institutionalized as the dominant social ethic—and idol—of American society, permeating every facet and dimension of our culture. White supremacy has been so pervasive—and so seldom challenged—as the fundamental ethic of society that it has left to contemporary Americans, both white and black, an inheritance of racism often not readily recognized as such. It has become so deeply imbedded in the basic institutions of society—in education, the law, politics, the economy, in religion—that it is taken for granted.

Thus part of the pathology of American racism is that almost all white people have been reared for generations as white supremacists and do not even realize it. There are, of course, some white citizens—like the Klan terrorists—for whom racism has become a kind of moral insanity. It takes no discernment, either for them or for others, to recognize *their* racism. What is much more typical, and much more important, is the less brutal, apparently more benign, but equally oppressive racism shown in the entrenched and practiced paternalism of the overwhelming multitudes of whites. The racism of the terrorists is acknowledged as abnormal and socially destructive, at least, but condescension is a form of white supremacy generally thought to be both desirable and normative.

Racism as Social Identity

Whatever the aesthetic differences between the terrorists and the paternalists, there is little moral distinction between the two so far as the idolatry of race is concerned. Idolatrous racism represents the assertion of the social identity of one race based upon the denigration of the humanity of other races. As idolatry (that is, literally, as a

40

worship of death), racism is pathetic because the denial or humiliation of the humanity of other men always involves the disavowal of dishonoring of the humanity of the person who thus assaults the humanity of others.

Theologically, the issue is aptly put in what Galatians names as the fulfillment of the whole law of the Word of God: the love of another as one loves himself. More often than not that passage is recited in sanctuaries as a sentimental aphorism, and just as frequently the love of which it speaks is confused with feelings of spontaneous attraction or easy affection. In fact, it is a most hard saying, saved from superficiality because it is focused upon the love of self as that which both precedes and makes possible the love of another. In the Gospel, it is only the man who is reconciled with and within himself who is free and able to be reconciled with other men. In Christ, it is only the man who welcomes and embraces the gift of his own humanity who can recognize and affirm the humanity of any other man. Hence the racist, grasping at an identity based on ridiculing the humanity of men of different races, is essentially, and poignantly, in the position of repudiating his own humanity.

His pretensions of superiority are farcical as those of any parasite. His grasping for justification through racial supremacy is a service of death so extravagant as to be frivolous as well as futile.

White Supremacy As Violence

White supremacy—and any comparable species of racism—is in itself an ethic of violence and has its appropriate sanction in violence. White supremacy in America is primarily (if not always obvious) a violence against its own purveyors and practitioners. Black men—and other non-Anglo-Saxons—are the conspicuous victims of white

41

supremacy, but they, and their kindred, are neither the only victims nor the first. The latter distinction is reserved by white supremacy, as it were, for its own kind. That a social ethic of violence can have no sanction other than violence means, simply, that the implementation of such an ethic unavoidably invokes the power of death as the ultimate authority or meaning in existence. Indeed, it may be said that death is the *only* violence there is and that any specific acts of violence are merely samples of death and carry within themselves the threat of death. (That is why, of course, anger is accounted as the moral equivalent of murder in the Sermon on the Mount [Matthew 5:21–24].)

In the most recent period of racial crisis in the United States—remembering that the American racial crisis originated in white supremacy three and a half centuries ago—there was, for about a decade, from the summer of 1953 to the spring of 1964, a singular reliance on the part of black Americans upon the ethic and tactics of non-violence as the means of achieving social change. But the non-violent movement of black protest—despite some particular exceptions that can be mentioned and honored—was essentially rejected and routed as a viable recourse for social revolution in the United States. It was rejected and overcome by an overwhelming white violence which, by and large, the established churches countenanced. The stoning of Martin Luther King and his people when they entered Chicago in the summer of 1966 is as much a symbol of that countenancing as what happened in Selma when the troopers stomped the marchers on Black Sunday in 1965.

This same violence of white supremacy, while annihilating the non-violent black protest, has both preceded and nourished the riots which have been erupting from the black ghettos since 1964. This same violence of white supremacy is even now being mobilized to quash the black violence which is its imitator. It takes no boldness to predict that in such a contest, white supremacy will prevail. What, perchance, will be overlooked is that this ethic of violence has been so far extended that the suppression of the black revolt necessitates the militarization of the whole of society, so that whites are becoming victims as well as authors of the vanity of this idolatry. What the servants of this idol do not (yet) perceive is that white supremacy is, verily, a jealous idol, insatiable, not even appeased by the suicide of its own idolaters.

Issues for Study and Discussion

1. This chapter maintains that paternalism is a form of racism which is morally equivalent to the racism of the terrorists; and that most white Americans are paternalistic towards those of other races, and are thus racists. This is a theological statement as much as a sociological observation. Can you agree with it?

2. Is all paternalism or "Do-good-ism"—toward the poor, the handicapped, etc.—a form of idolatry? Idolatry of what?

3. If you are persuaded of the fact that racism, in any of its forms, always betrays the alienation of the man who is a racist from his own humanity, how would you go about persuading someone of this truth whose lifelong savings were being threatened by black people moving into his neighborhood?

4. Why is white supremacy inherent an ethic of violence? How can violence be either dissolved or ended in the American racial crisis?

Now Hagar is Mount Sinai in Arabia; she corresponds to the present Jerusalem, for she is in slavery with her children. But the Jerusalem above is free, and she is our mother.

Galatians 4:25–26

Chapter Six

Idolatrous Patriotism

MORE THAN any of the other great and familiar principalities of this world—more than the university or the corporation or the profession, or even race—the nation is a symbol of salvation for men, an image of the Kingdom; it is a facsimile of that order, tranquility, dominion, and fulfillment of life in society which seems lost in the present era and yet after which men yearn persistently despite all disillusionments and defeats.

Plato's *Republic* or Rousseau's *Social Contract* represent such idealizations of nationhood, but so, too, do living ideologies like Marxism or Western parliamentary democracy. Even Nazism was beheld—by the Nazis—as embodying the millennial destiny of an Aryan nation. South Africa *apartheid* seeks the perfection of what is heralded as a divinely ordained social order. Those who envision a Pax Americana—a world hegemony subservient to American power—suffer eschatological fantasies. Every revolution promises paradise.

This is an issue not alone for superpowers and other great nations, nor only where totalitarianism prevails, but, as has been intimated, for the smaller nations which could never aspire to conquest or imperial grandeur as well. It is not difficult, to take one example, to discern how the asserted neutrality and relative territorial security—and the accompanying prosperity—of Switzerland can be construed as an approximation of some utopia.

In one way or another, and, it would appear, in varying degrees, this is a characteristic of every nation or would-be nation. It is in this context that every nation occupies the throne of an idol.

The Nation As Idol

The sheer arrogance of the idolatrous claims of nations, perhaps especially those possessed of enormous economic and military strength, is so startling that the fascination of men with such idolatry can be explained in no other conceivable manner than as moral insanity. One recalls these days of the self-styled "divine right of kings." Lo! the white man's burden in the heyday of British imperialism was actually considered to be bestowed by God himself. Communism—in both its nationalistic and trans-national forms—asserts that it nurtures the secret of mankind's ultimate destiny which is being relentlessly and inevitably enacted in history. Some professed churchmen in the flush of Nazism's inaugural triumphs expounded a doctrine that this aggressive nationalism was indeed the dialectic of the natural law of God. More than one President of the United States, not to mention any lesser orators, have propounded, with sober face, the theme that America's extraordinary power evidences an erstwhile holy dispensation and constitutes proof of God's partisanship for American dominance in the world.

All idols, as has been earlier mentioned, compete with one another, but this competition is particularly ferocious where the idols are nations. Indeed, the necessary corollary of the claim that a nation is God's surrogate in the world is the invincibility inherent in the ultimacy of a nation's cause, and this notion is sufficient to rationalize any aggression, subversion, or subjection between nations. This is what every war attests. Or, to put the same thing a bit differently, as with all idols, the actual moral power on which the nation as an idol relies and to which it appeals in its practical conduct is the power of death.

The Equation of Allegiance and Justification

The same moral authority—death—which all nations serve even as they invoke the power of death against each other reigns over the relationships between a nation and its subjects. Indeed, a second corollary to the claim of ultimacy is the demand for idolatrous patriotism addressed to a nation's citizens. And, thus, an equation is accomplished between the allegiance prescribed for a man and that man's moral significance or justification. To deviate from the rhetoric and conduct practically recognized as loyalty to the nation, on one hand, is to risk social rejection, loss of livelihood, banishment, imprisonment—all of which are threats of death—or execution; while, on the other hand, it is to court eternal damnation.

In any nation, the norms of patriotism and, hence, the acceptable idolatrous rituals, change from time to time. In the American national inheritance, for instance, Patrick Henry is revered as an exemplary patriot, though to the British crown he was seditious. Today, by contrast, Stokely Carmichael has been widely and popularly condemned and his loyalty to the nation constantly impugned; and he has been finally indicted for sedition. Yet, I suggest, any fair comparative analysis of the social goals *and* methods invoked by Carmichael with those of Henry necessarily concludes that Stokely Carmichael stands squarely in the tradition of Patrick Henry, although his views are somewhat less radical than those of his illustrious forerunner. The canons of patriotism change.

Again, the elementary parliamentary tradition, to which the United States is heir esteems the right and exercise of the right of dissent as the very genius of democracy and representative government. Yet, within the context of the Vietnam war, Americans have witnessed a President repeatedly denouncing the practice of dissent by United States Senators—much less ordinary citizens—as rendering "aid and comfort" to the nation's enemy. In the same context, the demand becomes more and more insistent and, seemingly, insatiable that patriotism can allow little more than a stupid allegiance to whatever is ordained by the incumbent authorities of the state.

An alarming proof of this demand was the decision to prosecute certain well-known citizens for their opposition to the war enterprise in Vietnam and for their alleged conspiratorial hindrance of enforcement of the Selective Service Act. Any attorney experienced in litigation knows how often extra-legal matters sometimes influence whether or not a particular prosecution is undertaken. This is notoriously the case in determinations involving tax, liquor, traffic, and so-called "Sunday" laws. Sometimes those extra-legal influences are personal, or administrative, or otherwise. Sometimes they are political. The decision to prosecute the cases in point in the circumstances, I, as a lawyer as well as a citizen, conclude, was manifestly a *political, not a legal,* decision made at the highest echelon of the state. Such a political prosecution has as its transparent purpose the intimidation not just of those prosecuted but of other citizens who would venture conscientiously to oppose the dictates of the foreign military policy prevailing. The actual target of any such prosecution (which, remember, carries with it the sanction of the threat of death) is to discipline non-conformity to the constrictions of an idolatrous patriotism.

These are tender issues and ones which are very contemporary. Other illustrations, less sensitive to either the conscience or the viscera because more remote, readily come to mind and might more easily have been cited. After all, within the lifetime of most of those who open this book, mankind beheld the atrocious consequences of idolatrous patriotism in Nazi Germany. But our concern here is to identify our own idols as a first step towards freeing ourselves from enslavement to them. Consequently, we need to perceive the properties of patriotism become idolatry and the tribute which such patriotism offers to death in our own society here and now.

In any case, as has been already said, no nation enjoys exemption from idolatry; no subjects of any nation can escape the claims of idolatrous patriotism, whatever aesthetic or tempermental distinctions may lodge in this or that particular scene. For a Christian, there is such a commitment as decent respect and open affection for the country of one's citizenship. But this is not the same as a patriotism which is idolatrous and deadly. A Christian gladly renders the former—it is what is due to Caesar in this world—but, by the virtue of Christ, that is *all* that belongs to Caesar.

Issues for Study and Discussion

1. Is there any sense in which a Christian can say, "My country right or wrong, but still my country"?
2. In what sense can nations continue to be nations without destroying our planet?
3. Can civil disobedience ever be a form of patriotism? If so, under what circumstances?
4. Are the frequent biblical images of the Church as

"the holy nation" or "the priest among the nations"
merely rhetoric, or is there a sense in which the
Church of Christ is "a nation"?

5. What practical guidance does a Christian have, if
any, in living in the tension of his membership in
the Church of Christ and of his secular citizenship?
Is this tension properly that created by belonging
to two different institutions? Or by trying, as one
liturgical prayer puts it, "to pass through the things
of time so as not to lose those of eternity"? Or is it
something different from either of these tensions?

Formerly, when you did not know God, you were in bondage to beings that by nature are no gods; but now that you have come to know God, or rather to be known by God, how can you turn back again to the weak and beggarly elemental spirits, whose slaves you want to be once more?

Galatians 4:8–9

Chapter Seven

Idolizing the Church

THOUGH IN specific circumstances one may seem to predominate over the other, in the realm of idolatry the institutional and the ideological cannot be sharply distinguished one from the other. To speak of either as an idol is to inquire into its meaning as a fallen institution or as a fallen ideology. Fallenness, remember, does not refer to a wicked propensity or some disposition toward evil; fallenness is not a derogatory or pejorative term; fallenness describes an estate of subjection to the power of death which both men and things in this history suffer.

The Church of Christ lives in the midst of this history, in juxtaposition to each and every institution and ideology in their fallenness, to be a witness and example of the society of mankind and of all creatures liberated from the power of death. It is no platonic ideal of church which is thus identified; and it is not some esoteric, separatist, spiritual community which is meant. Christians do not have to postulate any "perfect" conceptions of church or wonder and worry about what the church "ought" to be. Christians have been spared speculations about the character of the church. On the contrary, Christians behold and affirm the biblical precedent of the Church of Christ constituted in the event of Pentecost as a concrete, visible, tangible, actualized, historic company. For Christians, the issue of the integrity of church as the Church of Christ in the world is not a matter of approximating an ideal or implementing any idea, but of fidelity to this precedent.

Characteristics of the Church

In the constitution of the Church of Christ at Pentecost, there are two peculiar characteristics which distinguish the Church of Christ as free from the power of death. Both pertain to the church as renewed creation, that is, both inhere in the unity of the church, bestowed in Pentecost by God for the sake and service of the world.

For want of other terms, I name one characteristic the "secular unity" of the church and the other the "churchly unity" of the church.

The secular unity of the church at Pentecost consists in the extraordinary transcendence, in that event in which the church is called into being, of all worldly distinctions familiar to men. Thus, according to the biblical testimony, on the day of Pentecost there are gathered in one place men of every tribe and tongue who are, in becoming the new society of the church, no longer divided and separated and unreconciled on account of their differences of race or language, ideology or class, nationality or age, sex or status, occupation or education, or, indeed, even place and time (Acts 2). Such distinctions, so esteemed in the world that they are representative of the idols men worship and vainly look to for justification, are surpassed in such a way in the establishment of the church in history that the church is characterized, biblically, as "a new creation," "a holy nation," "a priest among the nations," "a foretaste of the Kingdom of God," "a pilgrim people," "a pioneer of salvation," "a new race," a community in which there is neither Jew nor Greek, bond or free, but in which all have become one in Christ.

Coincident with this worldly unity of the church at Pentecost is a churchly unity encompassing the manifold charismatic gifts bestowed upon the church and distributed and appointed among members of the church, such as prophetism, preaching, teaching, healing, administration, speaking in tongues, and so on. (*See* Ephesians 4:11–14, cf. 1 Corinthians 14:1–19.) These particular gifts of God to the church are missionary gifts—that is, they are entrusted to the church and authenticated in their exercise by members of the church as means of witness and service to the world. At the same time, according to the biblical precedent, the efficacy of a specific gift requires the presence and use of all the other various gifts so that they are all interrelated and interdependent, and so that each enhances the wholeness of the body of the church. The diversity of charismatic gifts is not occasion for division of the church into sects or parties or for status distinctions or exclusionary practices among members of the church. The gifts are contributions to a churchly unity which serves a broken, divided, fallen world as a forerunner of the reconciliation vouchsafed in Christ for the world.

It is possible to speak of the marks of the church in other frames of reference which are both trustworthy and worthwhile, but it is never possible to omit these two marks of the church manifested in the constitution of the church at Pentecost. Other insights, by a similar token, can be affirmed about the event of Pentecost, but these empirical marks of the church at Pentecost cannot be ignored. Thus, throughout the whole history of the church from Pentecost to the present day and, as it were, for the remainder of time, the issue of the integrity of any institution, community, ecclesiastical tradition, confession, communion, denomination, sect, or congregation claiming the name and inheritance of the Church of Christ necessarily and primarily involves the discernment of these same marks of secular unity and churchly unity.

Idolatry and Indulgences

The church is peculiarly vulnerable to idolatry where its essential character, given it at Pentecost, is impaired by divisions, on one hand, focused upon any worldly distinctions such as clan or tongue or class, or by separations, on the other hand, occasioned by the misappropriation of any of the charismatic gifts.

The church scene in the United States—not to mention any other situation—is simply littered with societies and bodies bearing the name of church whose *raison d'etre* originated in divisions of both kinds. Among the American denominations there are not only churches restricted on account of race and class, but also by region, incidents of secular history, and cultural heritage. Thus, some churches in America have their origins in the world—not in Pentecost, not even in the Reformation. They originated in the colonial settlement, in chattel slavery, in the Civil War, in agraianism, in the conquest of the frontier, in the ethos of immigrants from other lands, in the flight to the suburbs, in inner city ghetto life, in the subculture of senior citizens, and the like. And if there be many American churches of which it can be fairly said that they are so exclusively secular that they bear no significant resemblance to the church at Pentecost, it must also be confessed that there are no churches in the United States which have not been so profoundly acculturated that their existence in their present divisions is a violence to the unity transcending all worldly distinctions known at Pentecost.

Often simultaneously with such secular disunity, the American churches have verily thrived in divisions exploiting one or another of the charismatic gifts. Such exploitation is perhaps particularly vivid, say, in the case of some esoteric sects distinguished only by glossalia or by healing. But the reality is the same in a tradition which has similarly perverted administration or education. In either case, a charismatic gift has become a divisive or exclusive credential rather than an enrichment of the versatile witness of the church in unity.

Where both or either the secular unity and the churchly unity of the church, as given in Pentecost, are dishonored and where, consequently, some secular distinction and/or some charismatic gift is idolized, the members of the church become apostate. As an idol, it resembles any ordinary principality or else becomes a satellite of some other idol. This was a variety of apostacy which evidently sorely tempted Christians in Galatia; it is popularized and gross among the American churches. The inherited churchly institutions in the United States are typically engaged in inducing people to join, support and attend church—described and disclosed in this truncated and distorted sense—in order to worship the church, not to glorify and enjoy God, and in order to enhance some churchly cult, not to esteem and enact the Gospel. The sanction for this appeal is a venerable one—the sale of indulgences. Men are persuaded that by serving the church, by spending time and money and talent on the church, they can accomplish an exchange for merit and gain a justified status with God. Yet secreted in the idolatry of church is the same futile worship of the power of death inherent in any idolatrous relationship. And from that, even when it is shrouded in the trappings of church, has Christ set men free.

Issues for Study and Discussion

1. What can a Christian do to expose, thwart, or oppose idolatry of the church? Can you give any concrete examples of Christians trying to do this in the past and present?

2. Does the proper unity of the Church require uniformity in forms and styles of worship? In ways of approaching the Gospel? In structures and ways of exercising authority?

3. What might a Christian do toward making the "secular" and "churchly" unity of the church more real and evident in his parish, diocese, community, etc.?

4. Is it good or bad for the churches that their failings are now discussed in public and their internal problems a matter of interest to the mass media?

For freedom Christ has set us free; stand fast therefore, and do not submit again to a yoke of slavery.

Galatians 5:1

Chapter Eight

Freedom From Idolatry

THE IDOLS which have been discussed in this book—church, patriotism, race, money and status, work—are but some of the more obvious and popular idols worshipped in our American culture. People serve these idols, and many others, to give meaning to their lives, to justify their existence. They are afraid of death—that is, not only physical death but everything which does or seems to militate against life: alienation, lack of identity, frustration, pain, meaninglessness. And so they grasp, as it were, after aspects of life which seem to promise freedom from some form of death, and serve them as idols. But what they are really serving is death, for the fear of death is the power behind all idolatry. And yet, as we have seen, idolatry can only lead to death in one form or another, to violence and dehumanization and also to the degradation or destruction of what is idolized.

In all idolatry, then, of whatever dignity or fascination, death is the reality which is actually worshipped. Death is the deity of all idols; every idol is an acolyte of death. Thus death is a moral power which is present and militant in this world and which is constantly and consistently manifested as ubiquitous, pervasive, aggressive, and victorious over all other moral powers known in this world, excepting only God Almighty.

It is this superiority of death to the moral power of any idol which exposes the fact that it is in truth death which is worshipped, which is beheld as sovereign, in any idolatrous act or relationship, and the idol as such—race or money or church—is only the ostensible object of worship. And, meanwhile, men who worship idols die as well.

It is a distinctive mark of the biblical mind to discern that human history is a drama of death and resurrection and not, as religionists of all sorts suppose, a simplistic conflict of evil vs. good in an abstract sense. For what is "good" is, basically, what is good for man and all creation—in other words, what is life-giving, life-preserving, life-perfecting. God, the Living One, is the author of life, he is on the side of life ("I came that they may have life, and have it abundantly" [Jn. 10:10]). That which is truly evil is that which thwarts life. And sin is any denial or rejection of the gift of life; an offense against God who bestows the gift. But the wages of sin is death, not by some arbitrary decree on God's part, but because sin is by its nature possessed of death, anti-life, death-dealing, both to the sinner and in the various kinds of death it occasions in the world. The conflict between good and evil, then, is no *mere* matter of choosing between right and wrong; and sin is not the *mere* misfortune of the wrong choice. These are aspects of the essential conflict between life and death, which God has made into a drama of death and resurrection.

In the light of the Gospel, every life, every person, every event, is included in the context of death and resurrection—of death and the resurrection of life, of death and transcending the power of death. As death is not just something which each of us must eventually face, but a power at work here and now, so the power of the resurrection is neither something remote nor merely promissory.

The resurrection of Jesus Christ means the available power of God confronting and transcending the power of death here and now in the daily realities of our lives.

As the Epistle to the Hebrews tells us, Christ "himself likewise partook of the same nature [as ourselves], that through death he might destroy him who has the power of death, that is, the devil, and deliver all those who through fear of death were subject to lifelong bondage" (2:14–15). Men need no longer fear the power of death, and so we need no longer serve any idols. The resurrection constitutes freedom for men from all idolatries, whether of race or money or church or whatever. It constitutes freedom from death as a moral power in history, freedom to welcome and honor life as a gift, freedom to live by grace, unburdened by the anxiety for justification which enslaves men to idols.

In this freedom, we can begin to be faithful to our own humanity, and so faithful to God. We can go to work to give back to our various idols their true nature and purpose in relation to human beings and human living: to love our country and try to restore it to a sense of its true vocation in the family of nations; to use money as a medium facilitating equable exchange of goods and services; and try to get it so used in our society and in our world, and so on.

In this freedom, we no longer serve idols in our work or other experiences; we serve the living God. We work in the service of life, for ourselves and our fellow men. We work to re-establish human life in our relationships with ourselves and others and things in our society, anticipating in hope the final restoration when God will be "all in all."

Thus work takes on the character of worship "in spirit and in truth," and in our worship we celebrate the life and restoration we are working for. In such freedom, then, the present obvious dichotomy between what Christians do in the sanctuary and what they do in society can be done away with. What is affirmed and enacted in our corporate liturgical worship is what we affirm and work for in our daily lives. In both, we celebrate the gift of life as such by participation in God's affirmation of life in the face of death.

Issues for Study and Discussion

1. Can you trace the workings of the power of death in the present idolization of sex? Of middle-class family life? How should our faith in the resurrection and freedom it should give us affect our attitude and actions concerning the realities of human sexuality and family life? How about the idol of mass production? Of the automobile? Of "if we can do it technologically we must do it"?

2. Why must a Christian who is conscious of his freedom from bondage to idols always be in some way a dissenter in his society?

3. What changes would you see as needed in religious education (in home, school, church, etc.) to open out to Christians the present meaning of the resurrection and the impact it should have on their lives?

4. Can you cite any examples of men or of communities which seem to be living "in the power of the resurrection"?